THE YEAR OF YELLOW BUTTERFLIES

Other Books by Joanna Fuhrman

Freud in Brooklyn
Ugh Ugh Ocean
Moraine
Pageant
The Emotive Function

THE YEAR OF YELLOW BUTTERFLIES

Joanna Fuhrman

Hanging Loose Press
Brooklyn, New York

Published by Hanging Loose Press, 231 Wyckoff Street, Brooklyn, New York 11217-2208. All rights reserved. No part of this book may be reproduced without the publisher's written permission, except for brief quotations in reviews.

www.hangingloosepress.com

Printed in the United States of America
10 9 8 7 6 5 4 3 2 1

Cover art: *While You Were Sleeping* by Su Blackwell. Cover design by David Borchart, with additional design by Marie Carter.

Acknowledgments appear on page 89.

ISBN: 978-1934909-45-4

Library of Congress cataloging-in-publication number available on request.

TABLE OF CONTENTS

The Greatest Threat

The Year of Yellow Butterflies

My Life as an Idea

THE GREATEST THREAT

THE GREATEST THREAT

Here is a bunny rabbit.

Try kissing it. Feel the fur
around its tiny lips.

This might work better
in a poem than in life.

Real life isn't all about
frolicking in idea fields.

Try sleeping or taking
a break. Try walking

a few miles in comfortable
shoes. Breathe with your left

lung, then with your
right. Try not to notice

the difference. It may be
that the greatest threat

to hairstyles is wind.
The greatest threat to

understanding is bulbous
picnickers with cell phones

attached to their surgically
enhanced assholes. I think

it would be better to be
a bunny, not just any

bunny, but the stuffed kind
that flies over Christmas displays

at the mall, the kind that
for a moment lets you

forgive the bright orange lips
of the bright orange clerk as

she asks you to sign the receipt,
the kind of rabbit that turns the echo

of an auto-tuned note into the whisper
of a cloud-clarinet, into puffy

time marshmallows, into yellow
handshakes and yellower verbs.

Trigger Guard

Everyone I ever loved is standing
on a platform with a gun.

In the cartoon version, a flag pops
with the word *bang*.

In the soap opera version,
my face turns the color of merlot.

In the haiku version,
metal gleams in the narrow shadow.

In the Republican version,
two guns wrap themselves in a single flag.

In the Langpo version.
idolatry yips yaps paradigm the.

In my diary version,
I wonder why everyone hates me.

In the indie film version,
a gun flickers over a mumbled tune.

In the Chekhov version,
(well, you already know.)

In the 10 o'clock news version,
the crisis in violence is rising.

In the action film version,
a shot means profits are rolling.

In the catalog version,
the smoke's hue is a burnished moss.

In the teen movie version,
a nerdy gun removes her glasses.

In the lucid dream version,
I kiss a muzzle and it blossoms.

In the music video version,
a gun turns into a mouth.

GIRL 38

I had suspected
one of my breasts

had wandered off,
but didn't mind,

didn't notice
the nipple

poking its eye
from my ass

until you
asked me

its name.

\#

We call it racing
or we call it talk.

We call it a body
or we call it home.

I don't know
the difference,

if there *is*
a difference,

so say nothing
and wear

the extra feet
as a necklace,

high heels
dangling

like long
pink teeth.

#

A swarm of
one-inch

gibbering
harps orbit

what's left
of my limbs.

I miss them
even when

they're
here.

New Eyes for the New Year

The eyes on a face have brought me sadness:
the right eye searching for seams in ripped fishnets;
the left eye lost and wandering the dark; the eye
of the baby god crawling behind a couch in the moist
suburb where we planned our escape from video games
and grilled cheese; the eye of a whale we met in a dream
who spit us out so we could make the 8 o'clock screening
of *On Golden Pond*; the eye of the clock, blinking
when the oboe wailed like a burning shofar; the eye
inside the eye, curled up—a sprouting lima bean,
remembering the nineteenth century, those rosy drapes;
the eyes of missing fingertips, of sad afternoons
in French cafés in Dayton, Ohio; the eyes on the very
real parrot who sits on the shoulders of a wax actor
dressed as a pirate; the eyes of an actress pretending
to be my mom; the eyes of my father, sleeping on a train,
dreaming about miniature crashing planes; the eyes
of a swimming pool, looking up or down everyone's
swimsuits and into their souls; the eyes in love
songs written by mean men; the eyes in the painting
lost in a fire where we tried to save the ancient cat;
the eyes underneath tap shoes clicking like teeth;
the eyes of Fred Astaire, never blinking, even to kiss
in the dark; the eyes of the state of Texas secretly
tattooed on everyone's ass, and the eyes on the billboard,
ripped and faded from rain like the eyes of the best waitress
on the Upper West Side who knows everyone's order,
even those of customers she's never met.
Can you hear the eyes under my eyes?
They steal other people's dreams and use them for ad copy.
Here are the eyes of a man who'd be my husband if he
hadn't married my twin, and there are the eyes of the judge
who divorced them, blue as his tie. I forget the eye color
of the first man I loved—what color was my hat when we cried
in the snow? The whites of everyone's eyes swirl together

in silent music. Nothing like the closed eyes of a flamenco dancer,
eating a dripping hamburger by the highway. Instead it is
the right eye of a teacher when she touches her student;
the eyes inside my mouth and the eyes outside your mouth;
the eyes of the writer and reader, a broken vase and a whole petal;
the eyes on what you thought of as a cunt and the eyes
on what I thought of as a cock; the small eyes on the open book
and the bigger eyes of the closed book; the eyes I swallow
when we talk, and the eyes that fly above us in sleep.

Cybergeddons

       A woozy relic   live-streams
a private apocalypse.

       You try to forget
       the womb's tundras:

       their
           skyward

expanding cemeteries.

\#

Try to be the technician
           of flammable whammies.

Try the mission alligator,

           the almost inevitable
           audible pineapple.

\#

         The sand collects
         in ears.

             The beach burrows
             ravenous eyebrows.

Even if everything
is tired

        I still want this:

        some breath
        an unbroken ungunnable   *if.*

DEAR NOVEMBER,

I'd like to order another November
instead of you. There's some rain
in my shoes and it's flooding this
poem, turning all the gutters into
used-up guts. A fireman with an ancient
harpoon wanders the parallelograms
of Virgil's internet looking to be liked.
Is there anything less lyric than
a woman in orthopedic shoes, arguing
with the bus driver about expired
transfer tickets? We had wanted to
measure the starlight directly, but
ended up needing our tongues, which
had been replaced with metal depressors
and expanding space. Other Novembers
have comelier edges. Their insides
are kind, like a pudding-filled cake.
If you want to kiss them, take off
your hair and wiggle your lips
at the red leaf abyss. I tell each door
I meet to open, and magically they do,
when I push them and dangle my nosegay
in their burgeoning allergy territory.
Is that a fish jumping from the ocean
onto your face? Is your memory pixelated
by longing or loss? We salvaged fragments
of radish-motif wallpaper to hide in our
pockets for when the nostalgia police
arrive to ask us for youth. It's possible
Tom Hanks' beard holds an oracle that
knows why your boyfriend would give
you a dead fern for your birthday instead
of a yacht. It's possible music is glass
we forgot to look through. In another
picture, Sigmund Freud cries over

a lake-filled ironing board, or is that
the toddler Picasso in eyeglasses and facial
hair make-up? Everything we knew is less
than we know. An elephant places his trunk
in his mouth to mimic some words in Korean.
He's using language as a social function,
not to communicate. When we sleep,
the blue mountain lowers its head to enter
the multi-story houseboat with its giant
rocking rooms. Wink now if you believe me
and breathe in the cloud karate, sucker.
I like to defriend people. What about you?

I Love You Anyway

No, that's not me in that stupid
"Town Square" Doublemint commercial.

No, my sister is not a chipmunk,
she just has a *huge* gobstopper in her mouth.

No, that's not perspective messing with you,
that icicle really was about 20-30 feet tall.

No, that's not a typo; it's a book
about beets. Like, the vegetable.

No, that's not my head
in a block of ice.

No, that's not *my* wolf in the picture.
I don't "own" a wolf.

No, that's not a lovelorn butter knife
repeatedly stabbing me in the neck.

(It just feels that way.)

No, that's not the name of a song.
Only the Beatles can make a song.

No, that's not a superhero up there.
That's the latest version of 2.853 X.

No, that's not Grandpa, honey.
Grandpa doesn't have a monkey.

No, those aren't mountains undulating
and obstructing our view.

Those are clouds, I tell you, clouds.

Jaw Dance

We cover monuments in billowing grease,
skin-to-skin context   in pink brigades.

You wear a helmet.   I wear two frog antennae
and a name.

      Don't mean it.

      Try to be all loosey-goosey mama bear

until the bones come back to roost,

and then
                who am I in this
                borrowed century of love?

A moon landing staged in a bathtub?
A loose tooth and a white bucket?

We seesaw time machines   and skin waves.

                Pixelate!

Kick the juice
        out of twisted necks

and zombie eye makeup   blotching out
the sky.

You want to feel me   where?

You want to slide
            that brain and be it?

The war on kindness   has been going on
since how?

I don't need to make myself a man to be
a meaning.

You don't need a license to drive a planet, so why
should I need one to steer
a mid-sized tuber of fire?

Even my pet donkey gets an occasional weekend to go
hog wild.

We all need a little flailing
sprinkled
                on our down-home waddle.

There are a million countries in that bucket
we call home.

None of them naked.   All of them naked,

blazing   with spit-filled
                ruffled fins.

The Letter

You asked me to write you a letter for tenure.
I handed over a fossilized pear.

Better than words, I thought,

until you left the conference room,
inchoate rabbits falling from your eyes.

As in most meetings, I was eating
a marshmallow shaped like myself,

which meant time was a little slower
and space a little bigger than you'd think.

I knew I needed to start over.

Something had gone wrong
when we started calling our

undulating nexus of winding ideations
and spastic limbs an "institution"

instead of a school, but what else
could we say after the donors replaced

the windows with X-rays of
their baby's rebooted brains.

I should have known the pear
would fall to ash if touched.

I should have known the pear
was too beautiful to be a symbol

or argument for anything but
itself, its own dry peariness.

All afternoon the committee
circled the black fruit, gossiping.

I wanted them to embrace its bare
fragility, its dry delicate matter.

I wanted them to see the pear's darkness
not just with their bulging eyes

but with every atom, every mercurial
cell of their alien and ailing flesh.

The Epiphany Was Scented and on Cue

1)

Your cowlick pointed south.
The windows expanded like nostrils.

We saw the outlines of faces everywhere:
on mountains, in between manicured shrubs,

inside a half-full coffee pot. Voices from our past
drifted into the mouths of mute newscasters and

made us feel America was going somewhere,
maybe circling the ears of sleeping children

or riding a train through lush woods.

2)

Stand on one foot while the world pretends to end.

The beauty almost hurts
if you want it to,

but it doesn't actually hurt

and the sun isn't *really*
burning you.

Onyx halo glue drips from the crevices
and makes us feel real again.

We can be friends once more.

Like when we threw popcorn
at the television at your step-dad's.

Okay, we never did,
but we talked about it.

3)

I plugged the bed into the electrical socket
and grew comfortable with the white noise.

The yellow balloon tied to my wrist
grew thinner as the weeks passed.

My brother visited often, carrying an orange
that smelled like gasoline.

You stopped in, too, wearing a blonde coat
and small deer teeth strung into a necklace.

We'd spend all day looking at words
without reading them.

You said, "The best thing about getting old
is no longer worrying about getting old."

The drapes crept farther from the window each day.
Stars imitated the tongue-nightlight.

Did you ever notice the radio flying into the wall?
I had wanted to call that moment *love*.

SUMMER

The host's girlfriend is barely seen.

She's busy giving away
wild animals to reluctant guests.

      I agree to take a snake-dog,
maybe an electric eel, but when
I feel its sharp teeth in my shoulder,

I start to worry about
the future welfare of our fragile cat,
the precarious order of our rented home,

and remember
I am supposed to be looking for someone....

      A half-wolf, half-elephant
cracks through the walls
of the peeling wallpapered bedroom

where my former student
in a fuchsia robe and curlers sits
by a lighted make-up mirror.

The shadows off elongated fake eyelashes are as dark
as the branches of an evening tree.

The hovering body of a fiery sparrow is almost
transparent,

like flute music or an idea.

I turn my back

and finally, I spot her
my friend, the host.

She's sipping rum punch from a martini glass;
her whole body appears to be smiling, glowing,

and I don't know what to think.

I know she doesn't drink, hasn't in decades,
and I wonder what's suddenly changed, but
then I remember

the cancer won,
my friend isn't actually
here, there is no party,
there was never a house.

KREUZBERG FRAGMENTS

A woman in red high heels
rides a bike, past
the squatters' playground.

#

Pretending to ignore
a child-sized

U-bahn accordionist,
an old woman

in a high collared shirt
struggles not to smile.

#

In the dream,
it's unclear:

is the hypnotist's
mind moving

the shards of broken
mirror up

from the floor

(*or is it just
a strong magnet?*)

#

When I step away
from the netbook

with Skype on,
my husband

in Brooklyn
listens to

East Kreuzberg's
birds.

#

In the outdoor café
a young child

keeps squealing,

so much honesty
and insanity

emanating from that

squawking
thumb.

\#

When you wake up in a stranger's bed
with knife-sized needles all over your body

and feel no pain, you think
the hypnotist might be for real.

\#

By the Turkish market,
the smell of lamb and rubber,

a canal bridge
and a small, faded sign:

Toys "R" Us
now open

on *Karl-Marx-Allee.*

THE YEAR OF YELLOW BUTTERFLIES

Terrible to dress in the clothes
of a period that must end.
— Frank Bidart

You must remember that certain things die out for awhile
so they can be remembered with affection
later on.
— John Ashbery

#

It was the year all the fashionistas wanted to be clowns. The stores were full of hooped polka-dot trousers and pink horn lip-augmentation mechanisms.

Bozo temporary tattoos blazed on the biceps of every teen girl in a tank top.

When we first heard about the trend, we assumed it would be a hit among the sleek big-breasted co-eds—a way they could be seen without being sexualized, but in the end it was short, stubby girls who really made it cool.

Visiting a local high school, I passed one, a slightly iridescent African American in a curly rainbow wig.

After glimpsing the rubber nose hanging from my belt-loop, she looked straight at me and smiled.

She didn't need to say a thing for me to know exactly what she meant.

#

It was the year all the clouds resembled noses. Some were clean buttons, but others were dripping with cumulous snot.

We missed the variety of previous eras—clouds shaped like the Eiffel Tower or geodesic domes.

Once there was a cloud that resembled the schnozzle of a popular reality star—you could see the movement of the celebrity's breath mirrored in its shifts.

I tried to stay awake all day and night so I could record its trembles with my cellular phone.

I had hoped to post it online, but by the time I realized I had fallen asleep the nose-cloud had become two separate clouds, two unrelated nose-forms, neither of them famous at all.

#

It was the year young women wore blue jeans with carefully ripped holes, holes revealing leggings, and in the knees of the leggings, little rips, glimpses of neon paisley tights.

In the paisley tights there were holes, and through these holes we could see little patches of perfect skin-colored knee-makeup.

In the knee-makeup, there would be always be a gap where the real skin would peek out, and in that gap would be another hole and in it a surgically implanted transparent window revealing veins, and under the veins there would be muscles, predictable bones.

Inside those bones we could see little tubes, and inside those tubes there was the beginning or the end of language. I didn't know which, but I knew it was a kind of happiness like a crooked line is happy or like a million crooked lines are even happier.

I thought of it as a great yellow swooping, maybe the music of glaciers melting, or mislaid planets slowly readjusting their orbits.

\#

It was the year everyone kept forgetting their babies on the conveyer belt.

You'd pay the stork for it, then leave it right there, not noticing that it was wailing for breast milk or the past.

So many people forgot their babies that year that they needed to open baby libraries across the country. You could check out other people's if you lost track of your own.

I never bought a baby or even wanted to borrow one, but I liked to go to the baby library at my lunch break.

Under the mounds of congealing drool, I could finally remember my own lost babyhood—how blurry it was, how loud.

\#

It was the year Goth rockabilly manicurists applied mini-wigs to women's nails. My wife's nails were blond like a young Brigitte Bardot. They were half hair, half self-lighting phosphorescent wicks.

In the dark, I couldn't tell the difference between my wife's fingers and an ocean of glowing jellyfish.

I didn't like or dislike my wife's new nails.

They became just another part of her, like the wads of earwax left on the pillow or the glossy lipstick she applied after eating grilled cheese.

\#

It was the year people liked to make up words. My mother coined the word for "blinking underwater," and I coined the word for "sobbing with a cold."

My father's word for "ugly flowers" looked like a sick bird on the page. I could never pronounce my sister's word for "nonviolent murder."

On the train, I heard two strangers using Kate's word for "Global warming-induced sleeping."

What was the word for not remembering a word?

Some words were oddly addictive.

What was that word we said for hours on the beach?

I remember afterwards our mouths had a dry feeling like the taste after chewing old gum.

#

It was the year it was trendy to wear wool socks on your arms, but only if your arms were skinny and pale. My arms were neither skinny nor pale, but I wore arm-socks anyway.

I used to wear them to fall asleep on the old tuba my lover kept by his bed. With my eyes closed I could imagine a whole room of vibrating tubas, a tuba orchestra with tubas of glass and tubas of rubber, gold tubas and copper, tubas made of cell walls and crystallized saliva, enormous tubas and miniature ones, playing all of the symphony's parts.

#

It was the year those photographs appeared everywhere: big-toothed Americans smiling next to naked, hooded, bound dark men. We'd see the images printed on T-shirts, embossed on popcorn cartons and caught in the silver, cinematic underskin of our eyelids.

We thought that the image would cause a rearrangement of our dormant atoms, that the lion sleeping in our waterbed would wake and burn a rapturous path out of its oceanic nap.

Instead, the powder on our nacho chips stayed the same blunt orange, the ballet dancers remained perched, spinning forever on their lovely, bloody toes.

\#

It was the year everyone decorated the outside of their houses to look like the inside, and the inside to look like the outside.

You liked to wear a jumpsuit with an X-ray of a skeleton silk-screened on it. I liked to wear an earring shaped like a decaying liver.

Once I crashed into a friend's wall because I thought it was the sky.

We placed our teacups on a tree trunk ottoman and rested our heads on waterfall pillows.

You were wearing an ocean on your mouth, and I was dressed like the sun.

\#

It was the year no one could tell the difference between a poem and a résumé, a résumé and a poem.

I was awarded a job as a poet-in-residence at an insurgent branding firm.

I wrote odes to the C.E.O. on my cell phone and emailed ghazals to the V.P.

I loved the job because it included a free lunch with a salad bar and unlimited kale-flavored hummus.

In each poem I wrote for the job, there was another secret poem embedded in the first, invisible unless one touched it.

I was willing to let anybody touch it.

All I wanted in exchange was a goddamned kiss.

#

It was the year drive-thru prayer shacks popped up everywhere. You could drive right up, stick a dollar in the machine and watch a video of your future self lifted to Heaven on the back of a big-toothed gleaming winged goat.

The lines became so long a customer could listen to all of the *Mahabharata* on tape without missing his turn.

Soon prayer-rehab kiosks sprung up at every exurban mall. They'd hook you up in a gizmo that looked like a cross between a beauty salon chair dryer and a futuristic orange squid. Inside the device, it was warm and safe and soothing. Sitting at the mall's calm center, you could watch the crowd begin its back-to-school explosion.

You'd learn that subtle plaid is hip again for socks, that boys prefer their backpacks to be blue, and that little girls, they'll squeal for anything with feathers.

#

It was the year everyone stopped having sex. It started with a scholar in Beijing. She wrote a blog post about the pleasures of swimming rubber-suited through mud. Before long, an Australian electro-pop/hip-hop anti-sex anthem skinned apart the charts. Next thing we knew, a São Paulo men's group installed metal alarms in their tongues. Surveillance cameras appeared under the mirrored ceilings of Vegas hotels and inside the lacy polyester panties of mixed-race cultural studies graduate students.

There were so many ways of not having sex that actually having sex appeared old-fashioned, passé but not yet quaint. It was more like a fake-wood paneled station wagon than a peeling silver-plated egg cup on the shelf of a Prenzlauer Berg cafe.

I remember I was in 12th grade when people started having sex again. It was all at once. Maybe it was the charged air from Zimbabwe's nuclear meltdown or the change in frequency of the new satellites circling the moon, but somehow we all felt the need to touch each other and no longer remembered we had stopped.

#

It was the year everyone wore an eye patch as a form of language.

If it covered your left eye, it meant you regretted breakfast, or your childhood was full of big-toothed bullies, or you wanted to go swimming but the water had permanently frozen after the chemical spill.

Over your right eye, it meant you felt strong enough to swallow the bread basket whole, your funeral was prepaid at birth, your cat could read your mind and call the landlord to file a complaint about the broken oven that kept eating your memories and spitting them into the compost bin.

I tried to wear two eye patches as a bikini top one summer, but my nipple hair kept flying away from me.

You wore an eye patch as a jockstrap to an outdoor sex club, but everybody laughed when you took off your shorts.

I once covered my whole body and face with eye patches, so that I looked like a monster made of eye patches, a messy onion of dirty, flapping eyes.

\#

It was the year hipsters started using coffins as coffee tables.

At a friend's apartment in Bushwick, we rested our mango Bellinis on a neon model decorated with artificial feathers and rhinestone flies.

In Astoria, a co-worker had two coffins: one to rest home decorating books on and another to cover with hors d'oeuvres.

People liked to use their coffins to store out-of-season clothes.

I read an article once about how to use a coffin to brew beer.

The ugliest one I've seen was in the pages of *Us Weekly*. Its lacquered surface black as its famous owner's eyes.

The most beautiful coffins are covered with mirrors.

I saw one in a deserted field.

Every surface reflected the blue, orange, purple, yellow, pink, white movement of the sky.

\#

It was the year all the young men wanted to be ghosts.

The football bleachers were a sea of undulating white mountains; the strip club audience a twitching ivory mass.

To be a ghost was to skulk around unseen, to be free the way poetry is free because no one reads it.

When the department stores ran out of sheets, men started wearing white plastic garbage bags or deconstructed futon covers.

I couldn't tell the difference between a father and a son.

I started to miss men's faces.

I could no longer remember what a beard looked like or how one felt against my cheek.

\#

It was the year pre-teen girls starting wearing padded bras over their T-shirts. The lingerie was useful in its way. You could store cell phone chargers and banned novels in there, or you could hide a cherry lollipop for an after-school snack.

Parents were horrified. Some mothers hid their daughters in their pocketbooks, so they could carry them to work. A father locked his son in a Lego panopticon. Another chained his daughter to her desk.

Middle school classes grew smaller each day.

The hallways were so quiet you could hear the baby rats snoring in the cafeteria walls. Soon, no one was left in the building but the 8th grade math teacher and me.

He was a burly man and wore a live muskrat as a mustache. It was a broken umbrella in his hand, not a cane.

We wrote problems on the blackboard and breathed in the chalk fumes to keep ourselves amused.

Did he notice me staring down into the cavity on my chest, into the galaxy inside my bra?

\#

It was the year our disappointment was shaped like a lake and we all swam in it and your hair was the color of a fish's movement and my eyes floated in my forehead, so they were perpendicular and the world tilted as we tilted and the sky was full of a pale blue language we called home and we named our songbird "Money" and we sang *here, Money, here,* and like any other songbird she looked right at us and fled.

\#

It was the year it rained so much the rich turned their apartment buildings into sky arks, and the rest of us learned how to brew moonshine out of rainwater.

It was easier than I'd imagined and tasted like interplanetary travel (or an afternoon nap).

We'd get so drunk we wouldn't notice the wind inhabiting our favorite singer's sequined gown, wouldn't notice it humming the score to our favorite disaster flick turned hit Broadway musical or feel it lifting our imitation skin away from our new muscles and old bones.

It was the year that everything was so wet, so seriously soaking wet, we forgot what the word *wet* meant, forgot the word for non-wet.

At bedtime, we'd tell our little ones stories about the great drought, about how it didn't rain for a thousand days, about how there was a great man who built a great hole, a hole so deep he could climb through the earth and meet his twin, who thought and dressed and sounded nothing like him, but had the same DNA.

\#

It was the year us geezers wore digital masks. At first our masks mirrored our faces when we were young, then a slightly better, blurred version.

In time, our eyes became a little bluer, bluer and bluer, until the top half of the mask was an image of a sun-filled sky and the bottom half a field of grass. (I liked that no one could tell if I was laughing or crying or rolling my eyes.)

Before long, the young wanted to exchange their own faces for images of sky.

My granddaughter Jess turned her forehead into a midnight vista. The boy at the deli turned his nose into a pillar of rain.

It wasn't fair. That was our incognito territory. The young had their perfect elbows and unscarred toes to amuse each other with. That should have been enough.

#

It was the year everyone had dreams about nuclear holocausts.

In Laura's dream the sun turned the color of pomegranates.

In Max's, he hid under a couch with his pet hamster, Sam. Clara stood alone on the roof. Ken ate a cupcake shaped like a mushroom cloud while his friends joked about the end of the world.

From what I remember of my dream, the streets were covered in sneaker tongues, angular wounds, burnt moss.

I cried on the sidewalk with blue sirens.

What I remember might not have been my actual dream. It might be a memory of a promo for a TV movie, the one they advertised during breaks of the primetime soaps my mother said I wasn't old enough to watch.

#

It was the year we liked to wear opaque sunglasses so we could walk together in clarifying darkness and hear the clicking of light switches, and feel the shag rug on our blistered feet and smell the nitrogen circumnavigating the distracted air.

We were finally able to understand the difference between here and when, finally able to touch the sinuous gap between the meaning of *now* and the feel of it.

MY LIFE AS AN IDEA

The Romantic Sublime for Dummies

Think of yourself as a tugboat dragging
a star—no, more of a tooth. It flickers
in the mouth of the sky.

Somewhere an ego is dressing up
in a black clown suit so
the shooting gallery will recognize him
among the chattering orchids.

I was that ego once.

I walked in the blackest night
wearing a blindfold, braving
your water gun of coconut rum.

So began my life as an idea
and yours as a throbbing liver.

Poem for My 39ᵀᴴ Birthday

I am not brave, despite
being poor
      and Miley Cyrus does not
      give me advice
on whining techniques or
        glitter glamouresque
           eye shadow use,
despite my Twitter pleadings
      with her.

To be honest, complaining
comes naturally to me,

like reindeer ornaments
come naturally
      to aqua tinsel trees.

I am not kidding you
      when I marvel
at the appeal of sleep,

how I never grow tired of it,
despite so many hours lost
      under its spell.

What I love most is to feel
all the pillows
congregating under me,

from both sides of the bed

      and to feel the sun, not too
      warm on one side of my face,

when I fall asleep on the ocean-
blue picnic blanket, with my wallet
bundled safely under my ribs.

Unfortunately, most days, I am a little
too awake

to be completely myself.

The city is an obese rabbit
that lives in my chest,

slurping my veins with its mile-long tongue,
chewing my heart

      with its saw-toothed
               robot brain tumor,

and the laundry machine is,

um, you know,

         a laundry machine.

It's always quacking at me
           quack quack quack quack

until I
     whack it
         in the mouth

with quarters.

AUTOBIOGRAPHY (PINK REMIX)

Everyone's childhood was swallowed by a whale.
Inside the belly, we dreamed of a future where
we'd speed, miles underground, through the veins of
a snoring giant princess named New York.

Inside the belly, we dreamed of a future where
Manhattan would become us, but we would be
a snoring giant princess named New York,
shiny with orange drizzle and telepathic streetlights.

Manhattan would become us, but we would be
made out of the flames of other spiraling cities,
shiny with orange drizzle and telepathic streetlights,
our livers Chicago, our ankles pure LA.

Made out of the flames of other spiraling cities,
our noses would be the dirty canals of Berlin,
our livers Chicago, our ankles pure LA.
Skin: the color of mannequins. Eyes: black glass.

Our noses would be the dirty canals of Berlin,
skirting around Turkish ice cream parlors.
Skin: the color of mannequins' eyes. Black glass
hair lost in the mirrors of reflective birds.

Skirting around Turkish ice cream parlors,
we'd remember the sadness of our childhood,
hair lost in the mirrors of reflective birds,
memories found in the necks of oceanic monitors.

We'd remember the sadness of our childhood
how we slept alone for so many years.
Memories found in the necks of oceanic monitors.
Everyone's childhood swallowed by a whale.

Notes on the End of Thought

In a child's rendering
of my life,

I have a ram's torso,
a chicken's beak.

The cartoon bubble leaving
my mouth is empty, except

for a wandering comma
shaped like a tear.

#

What was that song
we sung to the eyeball?

Were you the song
I cut my hand singing,

my tongue cut my hand,
singing to the eyeball,

trying to sing.

#

When there is time,
we will levitate.

There will be time
to levitate,

to splatter consonants
on the ceiling like

feeling or thought,
to swallow atmosphere

and spit out light.

#

A creaky bird
remembers

his past
as a firefly,

how the woman
with the perm

tried to cradle him
to her plastic breasts.

There were no icicles
in heaven then. No ice.

#

When we meet
it's as language

(or as breath).

Don't listen
to the walls

creeping toward
the dark.

Peel away
the sticker image

of the river and
feel me, the real

river flowing
underneath.

Fortune Cookie Read Under the Light of a Neon OPEN Sign

Keep it clear and simple

like your mother when
she kisses and reminds you

of your outgrown stutter,
your once fractured knee.

Keep it clear like a translucent
lollipop, breaking

your teeth if you don't believe
in magic hard enough.

Keep it simple like lipstick
on the most beautiful gerbil

in the fifth grade genocide.

Get to the point and let
the mouths on the feral

strands of hair show you
which way north is and how

you can close a thought
you have already entered,

how you won't always feel
what you already felt.

IRemember.Org

My best friend in high school was Mona Lisa.
She was a dork! Dressed really strange and liked
to stand still as if she were posing all the time.
To be honest, I don't know why we were friends
really, but we met each day at the Leonardo Café
for breakfast and bullshitted around. It was cool.
She wore a necktie with her blue jeans which some
guys thought was sexy, but not so sexy that you'd
actually expect her to have sex. She always had that
look in her eyes, like she knew a lot more than you,
but was trying to pretend she only knew a little more.
Sometimes, in the bathroom mirror, I would try
to imitate that look, but I never got it right.
She told me once that she enjoyed skateboarding
in the middle of the highway in the dead of the night,
no one around to watch. This might have been one
of her lies, but I didn't care. I liked to imagine her
under the devious stars, her bare ankles reflecting
the moonlight, stringy hair loose in the bestial wind.

SELF-PITY

The best thing about this lipstick called Self-Pity
is that you can wear it with both active wear and
a couture chemise. Apply it slumped in your igloo
with your panda bear oven mitts and/or regally
in the powder room of the Silver Spoon Lounge.
No one will care that you spent your teenagehood
riding a leaf blower to the Model UN or that when
you stagger to the window in your stacked claw
heels, you resemble an elderly palm tree, swayed by
millennial breeze.

1999

That summer my strapless
bra kept inching down,

a disco ball piñata
hung over the ocean

(or was it a dance floor?)

It was all I could think
about those months, half-

eavesdropping as scruffy
men at paper cup parties

blabbed on about Deleuze
or the World Bank.

I wore a clear plastic ring
with glitter and a flower

curled up inside. Cultivating
whimsy, I was embarrassed

to be seen crying after
leaving my hat on the train.

Many times I visited
a friend in the hospital,

became obsessed
by individually

sealed slices of blindingly
white bread.

Song for Future Books

The book is made of glass and I look
through it and see more books.

Many glass books.

Is someone speaking?

        A muffled voice is telling me
to make soup, which I think
means I am loved.

What other kind of cup
fills itself?

Can there be a cup of cup?

A cup of itself?

Outside, a black squirrel has wiggled
to the end
of a very skinny branch.

When the squirrel breathes
the whole tree shakes,

as if the squirrel were the soul
of the tree.

Have you ever felt like
such a tree?

Not sayin'
I have.

Rain Turns the Sky the White of an Old Wedding Dress

No, it's just any old white,
opaque, regular as an idea,
or the scent of diet
ginger ale distorted (or heightened)
by aluminum cans. Inside

I sip lukewarm coffee (strong),
write lines for a poem I'll never
finish (shouldn't finish?)

      In it, a young
Shirley Temple, covered in ruffled
dollars, snorts
        powdered candy

with a round friend from
my Westchester youth.

The girls stay dry in the middle
of the public pool.

Jimmy Schuyler
wrote,

      People who see bubbles rise
      may be swimming, not drowning,

but what about us kids
inside the bubble or of the bubble,
made of bubble?

Are we moving? Floating?
Breaststoke? Butterfly?

My tarot deck from college sits
on the coffee table Bob and I assembled
when we first shacked up.

The table's legs are black iron
bathroom pipes, glued to a solid wood slab
and covered with ceramic tiles.

The shiny fronts of the tiles are hidden,
glued to the base. The textured undersides,
with circles in relief, are exposed, painted
various shades of blue and green.

On each illustrated card,
there's a wrinkled post-it note
with a suggested meaning written
in messy, tiny handwriting.

On the Ace of Pentacles,
the much younger me once scribbled:

> *Possibility of material achivement (sic),*
> *often $ made available to invest.*

WHY I GAVE UP PAINTING MODEL AIRPLANES

One of my hobbies is inventing games;
but I hardly ever actually play
any games, not even my own.

Who has time to roll the dice and wait
for the other player to stop smirking?
My other hobbies are easier to enjoy:

metal detecting on beaches, collecting
stamps that feature famous mouths,
hunting the fundamental laws of physics.

I also like to write letters to my pen pals
in the trees. Who among us does not recall
the sheer perplexity caused by the loss

of a favorite elf, or remember fondly
the faded periwinkle aftertaste
of a stranger's bulbous thumb?

This might be the reason why
my childhood is always suddenly
dying on me. One moment I'm

in a leafy pre-K eating veggie booty,
and the next there's a curly gray hair
sprouting in my alligator heels.

GOODBYE TO THE DOUBLE BELLS

Waiting is a bed without any sheets
or people on it

      It's also the light over the bed—
a little too bright, too clean

It's the sound of a chair,
sliding on wet tile

without anyone
moving it

a plastic violin played
by a truant monkey

When I say
waiting is a bed

what I mean is
the sun is tired

the cardinals are tired
the shadows are tired

so who cares if the moon
is friendly or not friendly

if my eyes are candles
or bulbs

\#

The calendar is on the floor
by the crumpled paper cup
that once held coffee

I have no career
I have no children
I have no plan

I carry my anxiety
like a red excuse

I can't spell
I can't make a cocktail
I can't understand
what my cat means

when she squawks
in my face

\#

If you are my friend
listen to the leaves

turning color and save
the sound for me

Open your mouth
and let me speak

in your voice
or in your voices

No one wants
to listen to me babbling

on like a walrus

Do walruses even babble?

\#

And so now, so long
to purple eyeshadow monuments

to the blue drinks we pour over
each other in the metallic night

So long to skyscrapers in black
feather boas with reflective knives

expanding like waves

So long to little girls with burning plazas
multiplying in their mouths

So long to dark men
with hula-hoop size nose rings

to halo static

to washing machines charging
into each other

like bloody hearts

So long to robotic hawks

and to the city made out
of glass corn flakes

to microscopic salamanders
we swallow and never spit out

Sanctuary

The here is we.

Shore lost.

Fingers missing like
the.

You try to enter.
And.

And so we.

No need. We try to
feel each other

without eyebrow
prowess

which never
works

despite the monologue
(moon glue)

you spread about
the we that

was or
is.

#

Under wings we hide our tools and remember coins found in narrow and
narrower hallways.

I wear a mask you threw off when wind hit the trees.

The children laugh like adults destroying happiness through an activated possibility of speech.

I can see their livers wiggling when they open their mouths.

They have seen the inside of all the migrating planets and like Earth best.

I don't blame them.

To hear a piano underwater is to be something like a child.

You can call your feeling "happiness" and move away from it and into business or.

#

Fuzzy wuzzy goes the emotive function.
Woof woof goes the moment of peace.

If you translate my *hee hee* to *ho ho,*
what is lost could power a drowning ship.

You said: I am looking for my childhood
under every goddamn rock.

I said: I am looking for sanctuary
under every goddamn child.

#

Brainy and curled up,
singing in the faraway look.

"I entered a language with both of my toes.
Now feel nothing but nostalgia for speech,"

said the punching bag
I used as a face.

All the eyelids dream of sleeping.

Mouths dream of singing songs
with only Os.

I am the O
you swallow

they whisper or the trees whisper
or the boulevard what?

Ha Ha, says the wind on fire,
which means we are almost there.

Hee Hee, says the fiery wind
which means we are anywhere but there.

The Wandering

We couldn't see   the sky-colored house
in the sky.

Eyelash branches   transmitted messages

better than a cell phone,
             which can't even translate

what the waves are mumbling

when they lumber out   of stone turtles
into speech.

And so we pushed under.

Forgot about the sky
         above the sky,

our skinny brains wiggling
         reptilian flute pills:

two bumbling faces,
      facing an abducted idea.

And Then We Started Again

I need you as a red panda conquers Minnetonka,
filling all the empty ponds with aqua vodka
because he is a god from another planet trapped
here when his intergalactic bicycle broke down.
I need you like an elbow, like I need my elbow
to be able to pick up a phone and call you from
New Jersey Transit and ask you the time. Always
I need you, even when the rubber palms pick up
their saxophones to play love and anti-love bebop
or to toss the schoolteachers and their stuffed
walkie-talkie jewelry out of the classroom and
into the revolving plaza where it is snowing
miniature white kitty-cats and gooey marshmallow
frogmen. Despite everything or because of everything,
I need you most when I don't need you at all,
when all the windows are locked shut and I put
my fuzzy earmuffs and flannel armor on, and
then suddenly find you smiling and lying right
next to me in our bed with all the covers drawn.

Not Here, Exactly

I found your letter
in the pocket

of a borrowed goat.

It showed me
the way—

small as an eye.

One mountain tried
to taste another,

then spit it out.

Your letter called
all the other letters

"friends."

You too were
my friend,

soft as a melting
or melted nail.

Dear little cage,
dark plum.

Notes on the End of Thought

In the park we think
we are in a forest.

The trees smell like wet,
sobbing tubas,

or is it raw chestnuts?

Your legs are undulating
unshelled lobsters

and so is my face.

No one notices us
sharing a single arm.

\#

All morning:
raw footprints,

a bumpy etcetera
I think is a self,

a detached, floating
compass needle,

not me.

\#

Sewn.

Sewn together.

Take apart and
taken.

We fall towards a we
and lose it.

Skin everywhere
like light.

He Is Opening His Mouth So He Can Hear Me

The old men are eating other people's eyelids

Nothing special

"Buy five noses get one free"

reads the teleprompter

Women in yellow nightgowns erase one another

"Send me the body of Jiminy Cricket"

texts the itinerant soul

#

The title of this poem was going to be:
                              "A True Story Ruined by Talking"

The title of this book was going to be:
                              "Truth Approximately"

But then you showed up with
your Coca-Cola eye patch

But then you showed up with your eye
burnished from looking

with your eyes   spinning like berries

#

Conversation is often possible if the lights are dim

Try believing in more to get more

The truth is somewhere between the pincushion and the nightlight

The truth is in the pocket inside the pocket inside

the pocket-sized coat

We fudge the truth to get to something else:

a love letter sewn into a jacket

a knife without a blade

But still we approach each other

And still we lie beside

each other and whisper

\#

We were studying history backwards

Inside the hologram, the real self—

a monotheistic toad   croaking for hot dogs

killing itself to give birth to   or   apples to another

Like a troop of ferries riding over the hilltop

   I say nothing and mean it
   I say nothing and mean it

tossed causally into a mouth

like that city

at the end of God.

Acknowledgments Page

Versions of these poems appear in the following publications:

The Believer : "Autobiography (Pink Remix)"
Puerto del Sol: "The Year of Yellow Butterflies"
Court Green: "Dear November" and "Rain Turns the Sky the White of an Old Wedding Dress"
Hyperallergenic: "Poem for My 39th Birthday"
Volt: "Goodbye to the Double Bells"
Bone Bouquet: "Fortune Cookie Read Under the Sign of a Neon OPEN Sign"
Eleven Eleven: "I Love You Anyway"
New American Writing: "Jaw Dance"
Quarterly West: "The Romantic Sublime for Dummies" and "Not Here, Exactly"
Hanging Loose: "Dear November," "Kreuzberg Fragments" "Notes on the End of Thought" ("In the park…") "Self-Pity" "Summer" and "IRemember.org"
Ping Pong : "The Epiphany Was Scented and on Cue" and "1999"
The Brooklyn Rail: "He Is Opening His Mouth So He Can Hear Me"
"New Eyes for the New Year"
Trickhouse: "The Letter"
Press 1: "Girl 38"
Hot Metal Bridge: "The Greatest Threat"
Maggy: "Cybergeddons" and "And Then We Started Again"
Marsh Hawk Review: "Why I Gave Up Painting Model Airplanes,"
Academy of American Poets website: Poem-a-day project:
"Song for Future Books" and "Trigger Guard"

The following poems were originally published in the chapbook *The Emotive Function*, published by Least Weasel Press, June 2011.

"Sanctuary"
"Notes on the End of Thought" ("In the park…")
"Notes on the End of Thought" ("In a child's rendering…")
"The Wandering"
"Girl 38"

"The Wandering" and "Sanctuary" were commissioned by Evi Jundt for the Lunatics at Large Sanctuary new music project, 2010.
Notes:

Some of the language in "IRemember.org" is from the memory website: proust.com.

The poem "The Greatest Threat" is for Donna Brook.

"Girl 38" is for Hamza Walker, after a sculpture by Rebecca Warren.

Special thanks to poet friends who read this manuscript and offered encouragement and kind, helpful criticism: Stephen Burt, Joy Katz, Tanya Larkin, Sharon Mesmer, Jean-Paul Pecqueur, David Shapiro, Rick Snyder, Yerra Sugarman, and as always, above all, to my husband, Bob Kerr.

I'm grateful once again to the super-duper HL crowd: Bob, Donna, Marie, Mark and Dick.

I would also like to thank the Pocantico Center and Rockefeller Brothers Fund for the time and space to work on my poetry.

To read poetic and fictional responses to "The Year Of Yellow Butterflies" (and to add your own) see Joanna's blog:
theyearofyellowbutterflies.weebly.com